Diverse Voices from Ireland and the World

the arts council
an chomhairle ealaíon
funding
literature
artscouncil.ie

Skenographia

David Gardiner

Published in 2024 by
Salmon Poetry
Cliffs of Moher, County Clare, Ireland
Website: www.salmonpoetry.com
Email: info@salmonpoetry.com

ISBN 978-1-915022-30-1

The cover photograph is owned by the author and features his great-grandfather Maryanowski and family in front of the family store / speakeasy in Chicago.

Cover Design: Judy Gilats
Inside Typesetting: Siobhán Hutson

Printed in Ireland by Sprint Print

for my mother & father

Acknowledgements

David Gardiner is the author of two previous Salmon publications: *Downstate* (Salmon Poetry, 2009) and *The Chivalry of Crime* (Salmon Poetry, 2015). Portions of this collection have also appeared in *The Flint River Review*, *Burning Bush 2* and *Poetry Ireland Review* and Salmon Poetry anthologies. I am fortunate to have received several visiting research professorships and grants. As the last student of the late Seán Lucy, I thank my friend & first student of Seán's, the late Dr. Robert Welch, for our time across from the grass courts in Coleraine during my U.K. Visiting Scholars' appointment at the University of Ulster at Coleraine. I hear both of their voices often. The Back Row (Decatur, IL) and Drucilla Wall (Poetry at the Point, St. Louis) provided appreciated generosity and the opportunities to share this work in progress. Very special thanks are due to the WFG Foundation (U.S.) for its continued assistance without which this work would not be possible. And, as always, thanks to Jessie Lendennie and Siobhán Hutson for their kindness, boundless energy, and encouragement.

From its two root words, sken- and graph, skenographia literally means "scene painting," which reflected its earliest use.... In the first century B.C., Vitruvius used it in a context which scholars sometimes translate as "perspective."

JOCELYN PENNY SMALL

Until the work *On Painting* (1435) by Fr. Leon Battista Alberti in which he introduced and defined the "vanishing point," these were the flat scenes through which we seemed to understand our world.

CONTENTS

Downstate Fields

Apeliotes 13
Samhain 14
In the backward season 15
Our Lady of Hibbing 16
Plains storm, Omaha 17
Wildflowers 18
Empty Beds 19
All the lights in my field are bleeding 20
The Heartland 21
The Blind Colt 22
Downstate Train 23
After work 24
Lincoln Service, IL 25
Small Plane to Memphis 26
Cars on dirt roads 27
Missouri 28
Lost 29
Remote Storage 30
All the clocks run slowly 31
Rearview 32

Night harvest

461 Ocean Boulevard 35
Canova Beach 36
Conscious objector 37
Gardening 38
NYC Garbage 39
Uneasy Pieces 40
These Dark Places 41
Frog's Love to the Scorpion 42
Found & Lost 43
Muzzled Dance 44
Autumn Comes Early 46
After the azaleas bloom 47
Normal People 48
Mostly I Walk 49
A Hymn to Bipolarity 50
How You made me, Lord 51
Gethsemane 52
Over Us 53
Third Shift 54
To the ghost of Frank O'Hara 55
Leaving 56
My Baby Bathed in Neon Light 57
The Innocents 58
Trimming Roses 59
Fourth Position 60
Night Reading 61

Safe houses

Lost in the Rushes 65
Bungalow Belt 66
Imaginary Mazurkas 67
Second Street Pesach 68
Glazer Baseball 69
The Lincoln Trail 70
A letter to Florence 71
Leaf Blower: Fairy Wind 72
Safe House 73
Complicated Gardens 74
Biopsy: The Stay 75
In my father's house 76
The Salesman's Son 77
Union Station 78
On a Belfast Train 79
Leaving Home 80
Maps 81

About the Author 82

Downstate Fields

Apeliotes

> the south-east wind, carried fruits of many kinds, wore boots,
> and was not so lightly clad as the last mentioned.
>
> MURRAY'S MANUAL OF MYTHOLOGY (1882)

The persistent line of ants is gone.
The fica's leaves are falling.

We'll make adjustments for the dark storm
windows, rain-marked bar-b-que, & trays
of finally dead pink impatiens on the back porch.

In time, I will walk this fallen world to the back alley,
line up the garbage in proper order,
& turn my back on all I haven't done.

In a dream I dream that Apeliotes'
winds make a new tropic—form to my wish;
seasonal decorations whirl the brown

marigolds, yellowed daylilies away.
There the common bed of dormant bulbs rise
& are strung: ripe twinkling garland around
what I've grown to call my world.

Then, all the three-syllable months behave,
the harbingers of inactivity
will silence themselves, send us to sleep &
stumble alone down red brick gangways.

Samhain

The doors open.
Candy comes out.

The years turn like corners
around the block.

The doors open.

I ask forgiveness.

The dead walk among us again today.
We keep our heads down.

We see what we want.
Those living among us are always

walking towards the dead.

In the backward season

The wind is cold through the sycamores.
Snakes curl on the warming ground.

I know I can see them. Beneath dry river rocks,
wrapped around broken hickory branches;
hear them, in the hissing smoke
of leaves I forgot to burn last fall.

Woodpeckers work unseen.
We other scavengers & carrion things
hack at the edges, holding on to the scruffy heights
& riverwash till the hawks arrive.

An egret, flying low, would take little notice
of our out-of-season pecking order

would land at his own behest,
disdainful of the cold silty water,
turn his head to branches snapping,
turn again toward the bad wind from the east,

probably, like me now, wonder
when his unforgiving cousins will return.

Our Lady of Hibbing

Grace is the patron saint of stupid deer.
Her white wings spread at night between headlights,
soar through the gray mornings over Leech Lake.

The problem is that you can't look for Grace
in this Minnesota town where we're not
tricked by thaws, quieted by August frost.

It's like we're high centered on a fire road—
solid old ruts through the iron range where
morning stars stay buried under March snow.

Grace stands in the diamond of light pitched up
between shadows of crossed blackened birch trees
& what looks to be a still, standing doe

staring into that limbo of sunrise
when the light breaks the horizon, peaks out
to disappear again under the dark

mined out & run over Mesabi Range.

Plains storm, Omaha

Around here, a truck's rumble past is
as natural as wind that rocks the porch swing in your absence.

"God doesn't give his thunder to us all."
We tell ourselves we're lucky; with our daylilies & dogwoods—

we're the stuff that survives, has roots & mind
enough not to stick our heads above neighboring flowers.

The winds, the sirens, & the early bath times
all fall together to make our long horizons,

hang together as the front porch swing rocks
with silhouettes of wild roses waiting for the storm.

The front of a life that blows in from elsewhere.

Wildflowers

Long, late April
in Nebraska &
I've spent the day
looking elsewhere.

Pulling azaleas away from the house,
giving them another last chance
for a season on their own
behind the garage, I grow to appreciate
all the dangers of lye, high ph in the soil,
minerals wicking off century old foundation stones.

What gives me peace,
takes their blossoms &
burns their roots,
leaves their branches brittle.

It's a sort of osteoporosis of nature.
That which shelters us
stunts the wildest flowers we have.
Even the roses will answer my daconill love
with black spot & rust
if I provide it on my own time:

In that July hour of the afternoon
between sleepy wasps &
wisteria fluff, when
the girls have gone.

Nature demands her schedule:
water early & feed in the stillness.
The wildest blooms we have
are stunted by anything
which comes to them upon any
but their own terms.

Empty Beds

The morning's cold enough to make
the sheets too warm to leave.
I dress straight out of bed,
the last to wake, long after breakfast.

One night of frost can change a season of hard work or love,
those things we confuse for each other around here.
There's a list on the kitchen counter—
"storms on house, cracked window,
quilts & comforters in attic."

Two night's frost has bent the yard to attention.
Unblackened rose buds caught in limbo
sway out under short, low sunshine.
The cherries cling near the dogwood.
The bees do their work slow, unperturbed.

I stop on the back walk alone in the cold.
Morning light just over the houses,
frost on shadowed squares of grass.
I stare dumbly at the impatiens,
four feet tall after a long summer.

The pink, whites, purples, & reds
lean against the house, bend towards the ground,
all contracting into two greens:
the dark green of the frosted leaves &
the light frozen stalks; both standing & dying by water.

I promise to leave their beds alone.
Let them fare with what dignity the season affords.
Yet what's left is convincing me to hang on to what's gone.
Though I'll have all Indian Summer to look
at my own dead impatiens', tonight they'll be covered.

All the lights in my field are bleeding

The Lincoln Amtrak service
runs between Route 66 & I-55.

The homes mostly seem stranded,
until November when the windows are cold &

on the last train out tonight,
each house shines with lights stapled to the roof &

a tree in the front window.
I think of the children, hearing the trains that

their parents have grown used to.
I think of the children as they ask for model trains &
hope that they hear my prayers sleeping on my window.

The Heartland

We live among the half wild houses,
trailers sunk in concrete;
converted carports

out here among the horse people,
tight hacking groups who burn their grass.
Their white-headed colt watches me

walking the dog, starting the car,
turning the blinds of our back room
at night, against the flash of a neighbor's motion light.

We're bypassed out here on Old 51.
Trucks roar toward Memphis
trains whistle in the 3 a.m. distance.

Not a porchlight turns on these things
we're not concerned with. Everyone's
at home. In the blue-curtained light

there's little to tell us where we are;
little to tell us that we're on the margin,
little to tell us anything,

until late at night,
the last train to New Orleans past,
I hear the one,

persistent yip of a coyote,
& roll again into unremembered dreams.

The Blind Colt

We were walking from the farm in Rathkeale.
A new foal wasn't feeding. Four neighbors watched.

I asked—caught only unfiltered mumbles.
The foal was blind & wouldn't feed. You said

we should go should enjoy our walk alone,
walk to Askeaton & see thatched cottages.

We walked into town. Saw Adare Manor.
You wondered why we weren't staying there.

Knowing nothing of this or your life;
I realized I was the one walking blind.

I returned to the stable, was handed
a shovel. The mare was alone in Rathkeale.

Downstate Train

Train through soy fields
frosted window & quiet talk.

The sun wouldn't think of coming out.
We wouldn't want it to

ruin the shades of brown & gray
that we own in our heart's & to each other.

We wouldn't want it

to obscure the crows' reflection
on puddles near the tracks

or even to make the water towers
seem less a part of the landscape

that we've grown from &
may never get out of.

After work

Everything south of I-80 along I-55 goes monochromatic.

We hunker down in our houses
color of a closed train station.

Christmas lights go up late & sometimes
forget about them ‘til we look up

one afternoon coming home to park in the muddy carport.

We add it to our list of things to not do, look awhile
at the broken porch step, plywood over the shed window &

motion light that never worked or maybe
no one has moved enough for its attention.

Lincoln Service, IL

I.

Sunday night train
black blue gray fields

All my thoughts are
on a dark blue background
Van Gogh's crows in the dark

Sun setting early
no cars on the roads, houselights dim.

Maybe I can see a dining room light on
a family saying grace with sweat tea

Then maybe too, I'll see Norman Rockwell's barber shop,
or George Bailey waving at me.

I grew up here.
All my fathers are here.

II.

Somewhere between 1748 & 1848, we thought we knew the score:

Work hard, have a family that you stay with & up at night
worry about providing for until you die.

They'll be women & children first to pick up the pieces,
make sense of the nothing that you made.

Looking out the train windows
I think I see families saying Grace

"Bless us oh Lord and these thy gifts"
for which we are still waiting & don't really expect.

Small Plane to Memphis

Wanda's drawl is so beautiful—
        "born & raised in Memphis, hon..."
That I wouldn't mind if she told me
        "we're all going down now."

Even over the drone of the props,
        the safety instructions sound like
Gillian Welch singing,
        "Down to the river to pray...".

Everything lately sounds like that to me,
        though I'm not anxious to be saved,
Or to meet anybody's maker.
    I'm at peace bouncing back over Missoura'.

Looking down on the farms beyond
        Springfield, I'm thinking
I can pray & I can pray down on each—
        Berkeley's God smiling down from a plane to Memphis.

My Captain banks hard north now,
        the woman next to me coughs in her sleep,
& light spills onto the arm rest between—warmth
        reminding me whose job is whose 'round here.

Cars on dirt roads

Two cars on dirt roads in Towanda.
One car idles at the train gate.
The other is turning in the distance
into their front yard with a gravel drive
where the train whistle sounds eight times a day.

It's just another sound of our nature
like dad's tired footsteps on the front porch or
mom rifling through the kitchen fridge to find
some sort of dinner after her day shift.

The rest of us keep quiet, wait for things
to play out, maybe not re-enact this
scene where we work, are married too young &
go to the high school games & our husband
works part-time somewhere in the off season.

Missouri

Everything flows through Missouri.
The canal takes the Chicago
River down there by design.

The northern Mississippi collects &
sends all that it can from Northern cities.

Even tolerant New Orleans
looks over her shoulder at the rest.

This gateway city remains still
in the dead center of nowhere

with no real desire to leave
from wherever we think it is.

Lost

I spend Christmas in Castiglionecello,
New Year in Naturno. I don’t have anything

but my myopic eyes on the world map
of my shower curtain. It's time for me to leave.

With the hunger of someone who will never
really be. I plan only as far as my suitcase.

With a too small wad of cash & an angry hope,
I set out on another adventure of all the places

I have to believe to see & very soon forget.

Remote Storage

I know there's a painting gone
a cinnabar inkwell &
some clothes gone too.

In spite of her hurry to get me out,
she seems incapable of saying goodbye.
Though, to be fair, I never really left.

I stowed things all over the old farmhouse.
Signed books that weren't actually mine.
My things became undetonated land mines.

She put herself methodically away &
I just kept cropping up everywhere;
albeit a part of things to be ignored—

like my books she never read on the shelves,
clothes that end up further in the closet &

a cinnabar inkwell that I left is a curse
because the scholar's red inkwell was made

to write love poems when the real work was done.

All the clocks run slowly

All moving clocks run slowly. Looking
for me through gym doors. Wave me
a kiss as I walk away.

The smell of my daughter's hair
kissing her & mumbling
"I love you so very much."

Time truly sometimes stands still.
For a father nearby; his child away.

Rearview

For me, the rearview is a side mirror,
driving away, leaning on my shoulder
another place recedes in the distance.

I can piece each of these views together—
a collage of all the places I left
in two-point perspective, vanishing point
that resides blurry in me & solid.

Understanding may be skenographic.
We foreshorten the bad. Watch it vanish.
The horizon is unpredictable &
vanishes into my only true point.

I drive along on the orthogonal
seeking some sort of perspective myself.

Night Harvest

461 Ocean Boulevard

They call it nervous exhaustion now—an easy familiar term—like
AIDS or cancer; a term repeated enough to take off the edge
until it happens to you, as it will, when you
overhear conversations in kitchens thousands of miles away.

The broken waves will whisper answers to you
to questions that you never knew or thought to ask
yet take you day upon day to try not to understand.

There's nothing exhausting about it until after
the three (or four) days you sleep straight through after
being up, but not awake, for maybe six.

Even then, you wish to apologize
to all those people into whose dreams
you are sure that you clumsily intruded.

One day, you hope & then one day,
you hope that you'll get your own dreams back &
understand the answers you needed questions for.

Until then, keep your watch
not nervous & not exhausted,
focusing on chord changes & the company
that you learn to keep with yourself,

vigilantly blessing the conversations
that you hear & the discordant music
of a world that you teach yourself to love again.

Canova Beach

Tidal times are on the news.
The surf follows its own rules.

Walk around last night's sargassum.
Don't try to count out the seventh wave.

Just as useless to predict the sandpiper's dance
at the edge of the tide, nervously at its sand fleas.

You may walk & comb for some purpose,
knocking over the same shells again—

broken but moving on & waiting as we all know
to be sand after our own breaking, to provide a path

that you might try to predict & that will always
wash away entirely on unknown terms.

Conscious objector

I was drafted by an army of one.
Sent to defend what I never believed in.

I walked through streets without any language;
earning my shiny badges & trinkets:
abandonment & misunderstanding.

No one told me the length of deployment,
why I'd earned a court martial for asking.

I'm guessing at some point, I'll look up, see
myself on a roof fitting a scope
on a rifle & what's left of my self.

Gardening

Trees grow, flowers that we don't call weeds blossom.
The whole world seems to be in heliotropic love.

These suburban trees are neutered –
ornamental pears & too fast-growing oak

Surrounding this aluminum siding.
But there are mornings when closing
my eyes & looking towards the sun.

I seem to be in order with things I don't understand.
I need to trust this self without being too centered.

For now, I dig & I plant.
I watch for the new annuals from seed,

re-plant & re-position the tumbling growth.
Sometimes, I actually climb into trees

with a hand saw & stupid hope
cutting away from the canopy,

laughing when I hold a branch that I cut.
At night, I look out at the silhouettes.

I don't know how to care for these things.
I don't know how to care for myself.

NYC Garbage

Shortly after their unsteady click
of high heels down the sidewalk returning
in triumph, shame, or hopefulness, garbage
trucks would come across the street below me.

My studio apartment windows opened
onto 85th. My bed was above
the warm easy early morning breeze.
I was a part of the city that

Didn't hide in plain sight. Friday nights without alleys.
I would walk out past bags on the sidewalk,
emptying out my too long work weeks.
On Saturday, I would wake to it all
being taken away—garbage, heels & her.

The hard horns of impatient crosstown cabs
told me simply to roll over again &
close my eyes. This Saturday morning
belonged to me as all the dust settled

just as I belong to this city right now,
last night & maybe again this morning

in chaos that remains all my own.

Uneasy Pieces

The streetlight flickered all night.
It was unclear if plows scraped ice or car doors.
A radiator hissed whenever I woke or woke me.

I could smell the down comforter & food downstairs.
A dish fell off of the drying rack at some point.

In the morning, I dress immediately out of bed &
search sinks, corners & out window shades
to piece the night back together again.

That done, blinds drawn, radiators turned down &
dishes put away. I might get some sleep tonight.

These Dark Places

I have shown you all my dark places—
rooms where blinds are permanently drawn,
end tables & armoires you simply sense are there.
The smell of lavender & cedar provides small welcome.

Your hands felt what your heart didn't know,
navigating sharp edges & silent spots.
Your hands felt what my heart didn't know—
that the room may fill with light, fill with flowers.

You have seen all of my dark places.
Your having left, I twist the blinds open,
sense the dust unsettled, hear your footsteps
down a hallway that I can't find in the dark

stepping over the broken vase, looking out,
I want to show you the flowers on the wooden floor.

Frog's Love to the Scorpion

We swam the creek together.
I took your love, assurance &
you to my heart.

I said I thought I had wings;
didn't know what they were for.
You laughed at me.

I took you onto my back
where you slept. I felt the weight
of your troubles.

I thought we'd nearly made it.
Then I woke you to yourself.
Then it went very wrong.

I made two mistakes with you.

My second one was my first.

After you stung me, we drowned.
I loved you the whole way down.
I thought I loved you still.

I remember what you said:

This all does not concern you.
None of it is your issue.

I hear this as saltwaters
hold me again warmly;
close around me.

Found & Lost

I run the found & lost department in your town.
We specialize in earring backs, birthday rings,
the one photograph where you look happy.
These things we find & do you the favor of losing

almost immediately, like ripping off a band-aid,
which, like that, you'll find comforting because
the first time you lost these things was a slow death
that you thought you would remember forever &

never forgive yourself for. So, we lose it again for you
& now there's someone to blame for the 401k,
the house or children, or chance that "chance of a lifetime"
that you can't remember. And now there's someone

sensical to blame, from whom you can collect a ticket,
smile & kindly wave as you hear the old bell ring
as you leave the Lost Shop & wonder where you
parked the car or where that girlfriend's picture is.

Muzzled Dance

1. Stigma

I want to dance
through the chemo lab.

I want to say
you should all "get over it" –

"take your tumors & your tears &
stop being such a burden on the family."

To say, "just cheer up,"
"it's all in your head" & "you're fine."

All these I.V.'s are near juice boxes,
saltine crackers, cheez-its & cookies.

Why don't I get to keep my shoelaces,
or my dignity, or anyone's support?

I am jealous of their acceptable fight,
taking on the scourge of the world.

They're all being poisoned, losing
hair & weight & perspective.

I wish that I could get juice, get attention &
be done. I know that's wrong....

But I also know that I know wrongly &
sometimes, like these, can't handle the business of life.

"It's all in your head" we are sometimes told &
it is & that's where we live & fight ourselves.

All these day hurts have no acceptable name.
So, it's always time to behave & be quiet.

A life of lithium & benzos awaits –
a life of fighting your own fog while increasing it.

No one can solve or will name what you have & that alone
can make the entire thing unstomachable.

There is no mark for unacceptable illness; one
so out there to be jealous of acceptable death.

2. Morning

I wake & wonder why.
Last night's prayers disappear.
I want to rest without myself.

Those who love me sometimes
confirm that I am a burden,
mostly via text message, of course.

3. The Edge of Sunrise

I'm at the edge of a darkness.
Read to me. Hold me. Promise me
that this will go away. It won't.
The sheets will be soaked by morning.

I'll be alone with a pillow,
lithium, small group & hatred
of either the sun or myself.
I don't like either of them much.

How does one go away from this?
How do I get out of bed &
pretend today will just be &
be different; that every pill

stops dancing in hated sunlight.

Autumn Comes Early

All the branches are hands,
reaching in our windows.

Scratching against our screens
obscuring the streetlights

With meaningful mischief
I don't appreciate.

It's a world in conflict –
with my peace, even sleep.

Leaves will fall, all might be.
I may even sleep tonight.

All the branches are hands,
reaching in our windows.

Scratching against our screens
obscuring the streetlights

With meaningful mischief
I don't appreciate.

It's a world in conflict –
with my peace, even sleep.

Leaves will fall, all might be.
I may even sleep tonight.

After the azaleas bloom

for Seán Lucy

Cold Boston August; two straight weeks of rain.
The white grutensdorf rose in the backyard
of the rented house isn't just leggy,
it's supplicate to the brick patio
that the University trims weekly.

This afternoon, Seán, I've read all your poems,
filed away with stained postcards & letters,
diagrams of "force fields," "language power,"
yet have only been able to note
that these gutters desperately need cleaning.

In the York Notes to Julius Caesar
you underlined years ago Brutus's
"Astute lack of judgment."

There's no food in this house & I am tired.
Your papers are spread on every table.
I wonder for whom you highlighted Brutus.
Then I see the rhododendrons were trimmed

properly & with care & though the one
wild rose has black spot, there's a chance something
around here will bloom in a year or so

in spite of our judgment, my dear lost friend.

Normal People

Do NT people feel lonely like this?

Do they look around wondering just to themselves?
Do they try not to know what time it is
so that bedtime comes as the entire day's goal?

Do they get frightened by opening mail
or feel ice form at every unknown call?

Do they wake shivering in morning light
forcing themselves to fake it & wake up?

Are they aliens in their own houses
& wonder why they still even have one?

Outside Union Station I saw a man
with a sign that said "Homeless & Lonely."

I knew him.

Mostly I Walk

Years of coming & going,
two or three months at a time

I still couldn't tell you where
D'Olier Street is or Angiers.

Only my feet know Dublin.
Shops disappear. I am old.

I remember back to no
cappuccino. Idiot

who thinks Grogan's is heaven.
I look for friends on the streets.

Another poet's dying &
I feel them whose universe

revolves around those who are
desperately in love with

their city I'll never know.
On these streets, I walk humbly.

A Hymn to Bipolarity

Let us praise the spectrum of words & be
thankful for the off-label use of anti-convulsants.

Let us thank all of the December nights
for the long, dreamless sleep that they provide.

Let us honor the mid-July sun &
three books, article & poems that we write.

Above all, let us pray for & honor
those of us who see neither sleep nor sun

Those who lived & live, stoking divine fire.

How You made me, Lord

I hear the wind at night.
I hear voices in leaves.

Crickets can frighten me.
Yet I still have my faith.

I'm told You're not supposed
to make mistakes. I'm here.

Maybe that means something—
maybe that I'm okay,

maybe there's a reason
that I hear wind voices,

look for You in breezes,
watch carefully for wrens,

know that You cared for birds,
know that on nights like this,

You look & care for me.

Gethsemane

> "Are you still sleeping and taking your rest? Enough!"
>
> Mark (14: 41)

The apostolic knuckleheads are there & resemble us.
They play all the parts that we are still too self-involved to see,
though we're not more intelligent than them.

They really don't know about the Father or that all our hell
is about to break loose any moment.
Only a parent truly understands that in the quiet

when you're having coffee alone before
you hear the tumbling of your children's feet
downstairs asking for things you can't do –

from peanut butter Eggos to sick days
to simply keeping them safe from knowing.

Over Us

Time flies over us,
but it leaves it's shadow behind.

I forgot the year it was
until I saw my daughter.

She was waving from the bench
at her volleyball game &

my older daughter was bored.
But she was patient & there.

I had forgotten the year
in the eternal present

I believe I spend with them.

Third Shift

Above the refrigerator's hum
& neighbor's footsteps on my head,
I think I can hear my daughters sleep.

Friday night traffic hasn't stopped,
the screens are still propped in the windows
& open the front room to bar close,
Hostess truck deliveries & 3 a.m.
grocery carts taking cans up the uneven sidewalk.

The neighbor always passes out eventually.
The light of his t.v. going blue on the brick wall.
Shopping carts in the same alley will disappear in gray light,
& at some point the humming light above the sink
will give way slowly to the more normal sounds—

the same cars not starting,
newspaper machines slamming shut,
& both of you shuffling across cold floors
knowing nothing much has happened again.

To the ghost of Frank O'Hara

> The soul has no assignments, neither cooks
> Nor referees, it wastes its time.
>
> RANDALL JARRELL

The cabs are galloping downtown &
all the truly beautiful people are gone.

I'm in love & sunburned &
we spent closing hour at the Met

staring at Hellenistic period coins,
Wondering why Philoclites is on a stag's head &

where on 1st Avenue we could just sit out,
on another single amazing night.

The full moon's up over the East River &
the air conditioners rain down redemption.

(Like I said) I'm in love, so who cares.
Watching this moon cross high terraces

we can't afford where people don't love as well
& never will, regardless of all their

summer homes out on the islands, I know it's
because they will never know our names &

their driver will always be stuck in traffic.

Leaving

Just the close of a car door
after a hug & thank you
can easily break my dark heart.

I've always wondered—
do my daughters know that? Not
the breaking heart but

the kindness of a quick release;
the promise that their lives will be

fuller than I ever imagine.

My Baby Bathed in Neon Light

My baby bathed in neon light,
Sleepless, staring for the dark through the night.

At midnight on a still, too warm late March,
I'm looking for something else to tell you,
Notice in the black & white of Ashland Playlot
That the shadowed buds have gone to flower
Before I had noticed a single leaf.

In the gray of an open loading dock,
I trace black branches on magenta skies,
Pray to the white-green moon of St. Alphonsus's clock,
Drift off to the sound of the torn chain net
Brushing the iron of the white steel backboard.

My baby bathed in neon light,
Sleeping, redeeming the dark through the night.

The Innocents

"All the innocents must be protected,"
I muttered, as you went to sleep tonight.

I tried to explain my pride in Michael,
my middle namesake—vindictive angel.

You smiled, stroked my cheek & didn't agree.
You sleep in some sort of peace without worry.

I've washed the dishes, cleaned the apartment,
checked all my mail, & stare off our terrace,

half expecting Commissioner Gordon's
Batman light in the sky; little boy you

know I am. But innocents really do
need protecting. Most of all, as your smile

knows, the innocent that might be my self.

Trimming Roses

for Olivia

There was nowhere for me to go,
then or now; the blank, empty sun
& long Omaha nights that summer.
In the rearview, I watched my life foreshorten.

I still feel in every quiet afternoon
their tears & arms outstretched still.
It's a distance that I can never map;
another distance I can only feel.

That whole first summer Olivia kept
the roses that we planted together
along the front walk—teas & hybrids.
At ten years old, my daughter knew how to trim them all.

She searched without gloves through thorns for
the three-leaved joints & the early deadening pods.
Throughout the long summer nights & storms,
she would sneak out with my clippers that she hid.

She didn't tell me until later & all the while
I was remembering the weekend she learned
to ride a bike & ended up in those roses.
I wish I could have comforted her those nights

checking for thorns & protecting her
the way that I did that day & always hope to.
She taught herself not to be scratched as she stared

for indications in the dark; places to be trimmed,
made to grow through her love, memory & attention—
my child in cold summer nights in pajamas & porchlight.

Her hands are mine. She tended to my heart
as she made the roses grow & held
my temperamental sheers in her hand,
returning them to the empty half of the garage.

Fourth Position

for Phoebe

Her teal crocs squeak on the gallery floor.
Her new glasses match the bell jar
of Degas' Dancer replica cast in Omaha.

"What position is she in?" I ask her
after we back away from Pissarro
as much to make sure that she has the right glasses

as that she might remember something
that I know after I have to leave her again.
She counts, tongue in her teeth:

"one, two, three...."

Stone City, Iowa is a gallery
away from us & I've told her &
her sister about 1930,

farm failures around here,
Iowa, why his trees look like
brussel sprouts, the stubborn idealism

that all will be well. I'm lost though.
"Fifth position!" Phoebe says now.
Her hands are back, chin proud.

I hug her, hold her big sister's hand &
walk through galleries of cinnabar,
heroes & villains of the 17th century—

all galloping off of their gilded frames,
towards some green ideal distance
where princesses dance without instruction
& good princes stand waiting in sunset.

Night Reading

Awake reading
nearly all night
when you are near.

You're in my room.
I'm on the couch.
You both under

the best blankets
I have left. Hoping
that your sleep &

my wakefulness
might mend & remember
when I'd crack doors

to the hall light
& watch you both—

mouths half open & beautiful
as only childrens' are

& hope one day you might know
I'm forever awake for you.

Safe Houses

Lost in the Rushes

It's never been the "Let my people go"
that appealed to me. The thing always seemed
a card trick of biblical proportions.

It's all Heston & Easter TV.
My own people came from everywhere.

Dad's were "marrying down for years," he said,
after they came over with Daniel Boone.

Mom's people ran their part of the city
within one year, opened a speakeasy.

I grew up knowing where I came from &
how much that meant to me, but more to them.
I knew that they all left without so much as
"Let my people go." They weren't princes.

Bungalow Belt

I was born, raised in Brute, Oblivion.
Forehead squarely between shoulders
& eyes on the Eisenhower's gray pavement
which has catapulted me across soy fields
& county lines, down lakeshores & railways,
into the state that only distance holds.

I come from a neighborhood where "regular"
was the supreme compliment, where my west side is
actually called "the brickyard," & the most amazing thing
was the Mars' factory front lawn, where a soft chocolate smell rose
from the only good-smelling plant our families knew, & where
the fat back tire of your banana seat bike was rumored to explode
if you cut the least of a line through those corners.

Whether the clay or the people came first here, I don't know.
Bricks were wrenched out of the quarry, I think,
already colored red & holed & ready to stack
up bungalows down the gridded gentile streets—
short, square, solid homes; short, square, solid streets—

a stackable foundation as easily lost as the imprint on a cinder block,
the address on the curb, or a shallow handprint in a cracked sidewalk.

Imaginary Mazurkas

Diversy and Mobile Streets

At night, I look for the big-kettled kitchens. Turn full from the parkway,
stare through windows, & try to lift a view from the gone beat cop.

Through a broken blind, I see the women running the home,
catch glimpses of their mute dresses passing open bedrooms,
casting shadows across the front hallway.

Dzia dzias sit in red-orange lumpy chairs, unread newspapers folded,
antimacassars crumpled everywhere.

These shadows box tonight with the radiator hiss of wind through dead elms,
the sound of truck breaks on the tollway overhead.

Sophie will wake up at four & cook dinner for Chrissy to warm.
Len will come home laughing & sleepy, toss a heavy lunch box on the table.
Adam & his granddaughter will fall asleep watching Gorgeous George.

The whole picture fades in miniature as I squint past my collar.
Windows steam & blue light creeps out. Through snowflakes the size of mothballs
The metal blinds are giving way back to those same lace curtains.

Turning the corner, I see the snow & petals of glass down the alley—
a sparkling, broken river of milk bottles from a tomorrow morning

that has yet to happen again. It reaches west beyond Harlem Avenue,
away from this small square of light & rattle of the past.

Second Street Pesach

They sit till sundown on Sunday, quiet
on the front porch in Springfield. Hands folded
in mute conversation & militant piety.

My elder aunt & great grandmother—
displaced Catholics, paternal observers
of the Bible belt, the tomb, & cinder streets.

Great grandmother stood six feet tall.
Her runaway sister would speak little, at all.
Her silence knew the Kishinev pogrom.
Her husband was still; a picture in the bedroom mirror—
in a prayer shawl, standing in important pose,
obscured by the lacey dress of the Child of Prague.

As the sun went down on Second Street,
they stood, straightened their skirts,
& went into their next glasses of wine.

They disappear with my crooked memory
past the mezuzah & into the same silence of the day;
the vacuum that all our pasts are becoming.

Glazer Baseball

My grandparents' pine tree grew through the fence;
Without that shade, the garage workshop fell itself.

The backyard became a great green straw mat
whose sticky silence I would shatter
on weekend visits with my whiffle bat,
flailing the air to the backbeat of cracking glass.

Gardiner's Glass Company was a one-
man show. Grandpa's knotty gray knuckles
put up the wooden sign, painted the truck,
penciled & etched each line in stacked, broken sheets of glass

laid over rug-wrapped benches, carpeted
sawhorses. Quick taps of the ball-peen.
Precise, lines branching out towards the doorway.
Sundance & soap bubble rainbows, he commanded

onto the back of his truck in measured,
kaleidoscopic, pot-hole defying,
three-on-the-tree order, in the alley
that was our warning track.

My grandparents' pine tree grew through the fence;
Without that shade, the garage workshop fell itself.

The Lincoln Trail

There were these sad cellos
playing along I-74 to Springfield.
I've never known a happy cello,
but I know that in our gone family farms
the alarm clock radio in the kitchen
never heard anything sadder than Tommy Dorsey
over the rattle of dishes on Sunday nights.

Hank & his two brothers were in polka band.
Grandpa's banjo was hung up the year Teddy died of TB.
At eight, I found a clarinet behind the storms in the work shed.
Without making a sound, I tasted splinters & dust & told no one.

Old route 36 reminds me of these things.
Just out of radio range, I'm listening between static,
not willing to give up on the cellos or the talk.
The road stretches out along dusty splintered windowpanes
that I place cobwebs in at 60 m.p.h.
It's almost as if you could play them.
String music that would slowly give way

To winter dances, & wedding dinners, & Grandma—
Platinum blond on another man's arm,
Decades before she'd be brought out here
To be found out, dancing in the kitchen, alone in mid-afternoon.

A letter to Florence

i.m. Florence Sherwood Gardiner (1917-1994)

They were cleaning out the Temple the morning I heard—
sweeping down cobwebs, folding tables up.
The whole parlor closed, & the quiet consumed me.
That morning I thought of rosary beads &

that mass is only as long as a grandma's rosary.
A given life only so long as our fingers
counting beads, snapping beans, or set squarely
on the round edge of a kitchen table.

That morning's reading said simply to me,
"I am eaten up with zeal for your house" (Jn 2:17).
I know your house simply as another
place, like others, I haven't been enough.

& of all the things that I think I know,
I know so little of you. Only that
cornstarch & flour are mixed for breading,
& when you were a little girl...something....

Your past to me,
despite the genealogy,
is the sandy shore of Tiberias.

Looking east over quiet soybean fields,
back through your five-hundred-year-old English name,
back through silence like empty interstates
to the creases around your eyes,

I know only:

The zeal for your house consumes me.

Leaf Blower: Fairy Wind

It's a stupid battery-operated leaf blower.
I get towards the garage, wondering

if I need to get another beer before I finish,
the dead leaves whirl in a taller circle & I wonder

is this really a fairy wind? Can a Black & Decker
produce spirits? The autumn leaves hit me hard in the face.

I get tired decide to go inside & think on the couch
as my father, like other non-believers, would have done.

Safe House

There's a house full of cats.
It's a shambles I love
of rooms I've never seen,
with water, I'm told, in
a basement I won't see.

Out of every corner & coffee table
creep cats & broken vases & fabulous things.

This is the chaos of love.
I listen to gutters drip.

I watch the backyard fill with clay
& cats' elevateds collect dust.

But by watching, I hear.
You saying anything
to me & everything
I ever needed to hear.

I curl into blankets
you have too many of &
the too many cats do
whatever cats do &

nothing in the house gets fixed;

except the two of us.

Complicated Gardens

Scott's Lawn Service comes through &
I think I can refuse to mulch.

I pull nightshade myself &
watch as my allergic welts come.

It's all for a flower garden
that my parents used to see

from bed, out their window.
that's what I contribute—

allergens & lawn services
where my father once hybrid flowers.

Biopsy: The Stay

I'm at your bedside & you're the only
one now who doesn't know that you're dying.

You're asleep but wave to me at one point.
I want to talk to you about everything now,
right now, before the doctor comes in late & then
tells you that you're dying.

We will never have a normal conversation again.
I'm wondering now if we ever did & why I hold this.

I want to stay this moment of execution.
I want you to truly wake. I want you to talk
to me & to be like it was two hours ago.

I want so many things but only for you to live.
For now, I settle for holding your hand & praying

That the doctor not come & please grant us just that—
an absent walking away of this bad angel.

You wake briefly & open & close your eyes to me.

I want to talk to you about everything now, right now, now
before the doctor comes in, tells you you're leaving,
dying & we'll never have a normal conversation again after that.

We never really did. I just want that moment.
I want you to talk to me & it to be like it was two hours ago.

But I know you've been hurting for too long a time.

In my father's house

In my father's house,
my mother lives alone.

Surrounded by whirling
grandchildren, her world

seems filled once again
like when they were young.

Only I remember that.
Eldest observant absent.

At night on the couch,
I see pictures in the dark;

weeds through walls in the garden
that I no longer tend to.

In my father's house,
there are many rooms.

For Jesus, they were
waiting for us all.

For me, they are all
waiting for cleaning

to come through & make
the beds & put this

all back together.

The Salesman's Son

You were my idol –

You read every book I thought of,
or even mentioned. Had autographs
from every golfer or footballer.

I'd watch you at home –

controlling the kitchen like
the galloping gourmet, short glass
Martini in hand & records playing.

My hero & god –

I wanted to be everything
you were & to you. Then,
one day I matched your height.

We were both tall, quiet –

I learned you read
The New York Review of Books &
read all of Faulkner only after
I called you out on it.

We were never the same –

Through your illness, I stood
by & prayed every day that you'd
come back to that man I knew.

I'm not unique in this –

It's the passage of all true sons.
We see in our father's faults ourselves.
We care for you onto death.

I long to idolize you again.

Union Station

I naively love riding the train out of the city.
Sun setting & the general tiredness of just work.

I imagine my father & his three fraternity brothers,
stopping the drink cart & playing whist on their slow way home.

I stare out the window & drink beer from a paper bag.
I live as an adjunct between day, place, states of being.

It's a time between where you've been & where you might end up;
a time between sunset shading alleys between walk ups

to simply & silently be alone on a loud train
in full flight from what might or should have been.

On a Belfast Train

i.m. Robert Welch

Counting Antrim greens in a gorgeous fall
in an Ulster autumn that I've hated but for your home.

Slow train to Belfast & I'm simply numb.
Ballymena means nothing to me now.

I've watched the same trumpeter swan crossing
that same second bridge in Coleraine for two months.

I don't even duck anymore nearing its nest,
hold my head high & imagine

taking a boat up the Lagan with Simmons,
then wonder if the Belfast Enterprise

really would go beyond Dublin, into
outer space & take us all somewhere like home.

Leaving Home

Someone once told me
you're already home
wherever you feel loved.

But we made that up.
It's a wish fulfilment—
that sort of felt love.

Frost's hired man died alone.
They never let him in.
He did things, was trouble.

He was necessary,
present, useful, just there.

Maps

for Julianne

We are walking a pattern
that we don't understand,
mapping confusion like a dog in the rainy dark.

Children & pets & partners may appear.
Presence & absence happens & is gone.

On the map legend, there may be names, dates.
Unmarked places are all over the place.
We make up those names & dates despite facts

after we forget the exit ramps, round-abouts & rest areas
that we passed as we look at, what we think, is

a metered straight line from the past to here.

Dr. DAVID GARDINER is a poet, editor and professor who was born and raised in Chicago. From 2006 to 2010, he was the founder & editor of the international arts journal, An Sionnach, which published Van Morrison, Seamus Heaney, Eavan Boland, Paula Meehan and Eamonn Wall, among others. He attended the first Writers' Workshop at University College Galway under the direction of Gerald Dawe and was taught there by Thomas Kilroy, John McGahern, Richard Murphy, and others. For over ten years, he directed the Creighton summer program at Trinity College Dublin. He has authored over sixty journal publications, edited over twenty five journals and volumes, and written five books, including the Salmon poetry collections Downstate (2009) and The Chivalry of Crime (2015). He is currently Director of the Center for Irish Studies and Editor of The New Hibernia Review at the University of St. Thomas (St. Paul, MN).

L-R: Olivia Clare Gardiner, David Michael Gardiner, and Phoebe Kathleen Gardiner

salmonpoetry

Cliffs of Moher, County Clare, Ireland

"Publishing the finest Irish and international literature."
Michael D. Higgins, President of Ireland